Whales

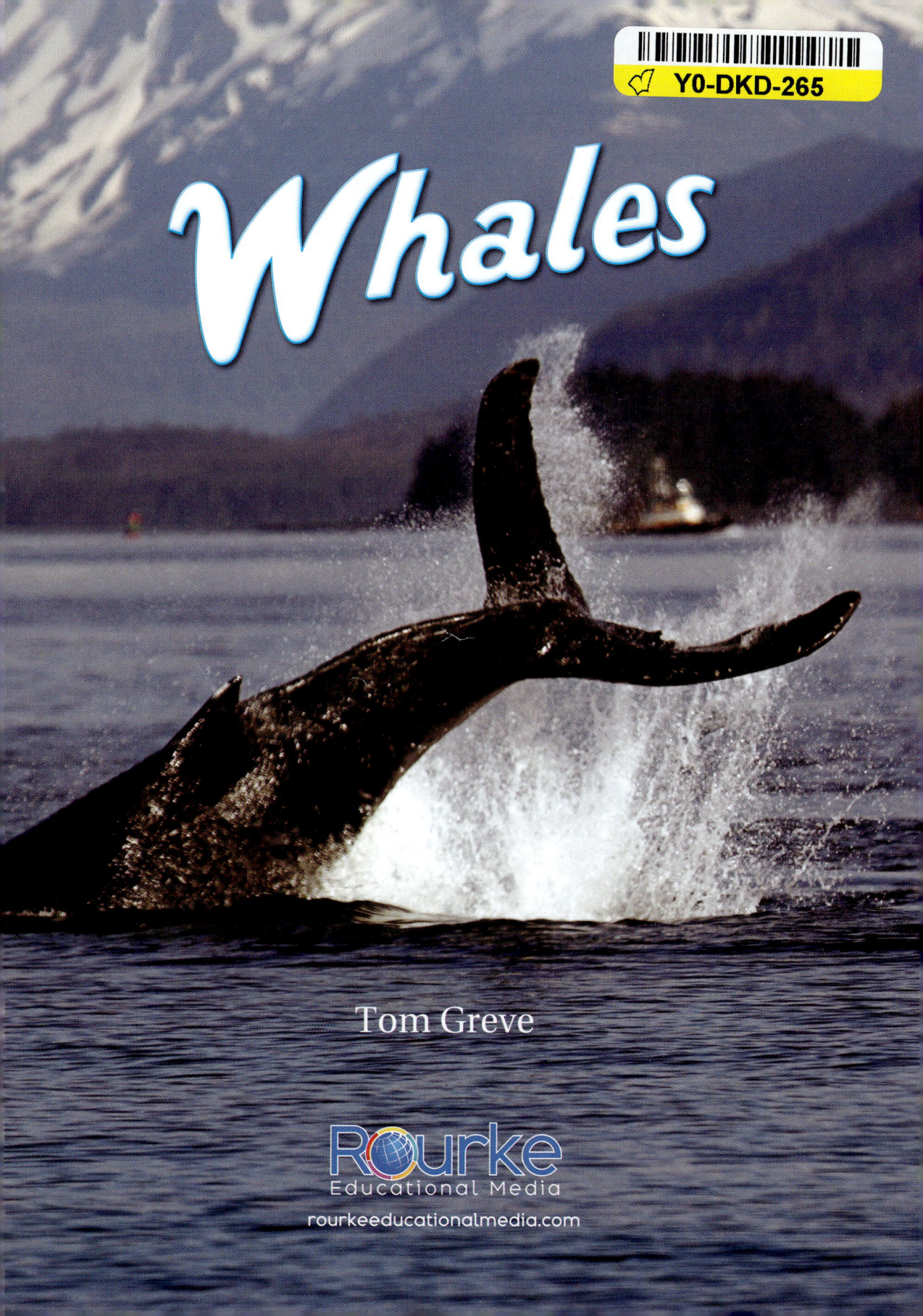

Tom Greve

Rourke
Educational Media

rourkeeducationalmedia.com

© 2011 Rourke Educational Media

All rights reserved. No part of this book may be reproduced or utilized in any form or by any means, electronic or mechanical including photocopying, recording, or by any information storage and retrieval system without permission in writing from the publisher.

www.rourkeeducationalmedia.com

PHOTO CREDITS: Cover: © lunavandoorne; Title Page: © ChadKruzic; Page 2, 3: © Metropoway893; Page 4, 5, 22: © Idreamphotos; Page 6: © Hofmeester; Page 7: © Montreal_Photos, © Isselee; Page 8: © Andreus; Page 10, 11: © Mike Johnson, Marine Natural History Photography; Page 11: © Buch; Page 12: © Library of Congress; ©Wdeon, © robynmac, © Wikipedia; Page 13: © IFAW; Page 14: © Elnavegante; Page 15: © Wikipedia; Page 16: © Greenpeace/ Walter Obiol; Page 17: © Davemcaleavy; © aurent Neumann, © IFAW; Page: © Mouskie; Page 19: © Freedomimage; Page 20: doescher; Page 21: © Jocrebbin

Editor: Precious McKenzie

Cover and Page design by Teri Intzegian

Library of Congress Cataloging-in-Publication Data

Greve, Tom.
 Whales / Tom Greve.
     p. cm. -- (Eye to eye with endangered species)
 Includes bibliographical references and index.
 ISBN 978-1-61590-273-6 (Hard Cover) (alk. paper)
 ISBN 978-1-61590-513-3 (Soft Cover)
 1. Whales--Juvenile literature. I. Title.
 QL737.C4G76 2011
 599.5--dc22
                                             201001010

Rourke Educational Media
Printed in the United States of America, North Mankato, Minnesota

rourkeeducationalmedia.com

customerservice@rourkeeducationalmedia.com • PO Box 643328 Vero Beach, Florida 32964

Table of Contents

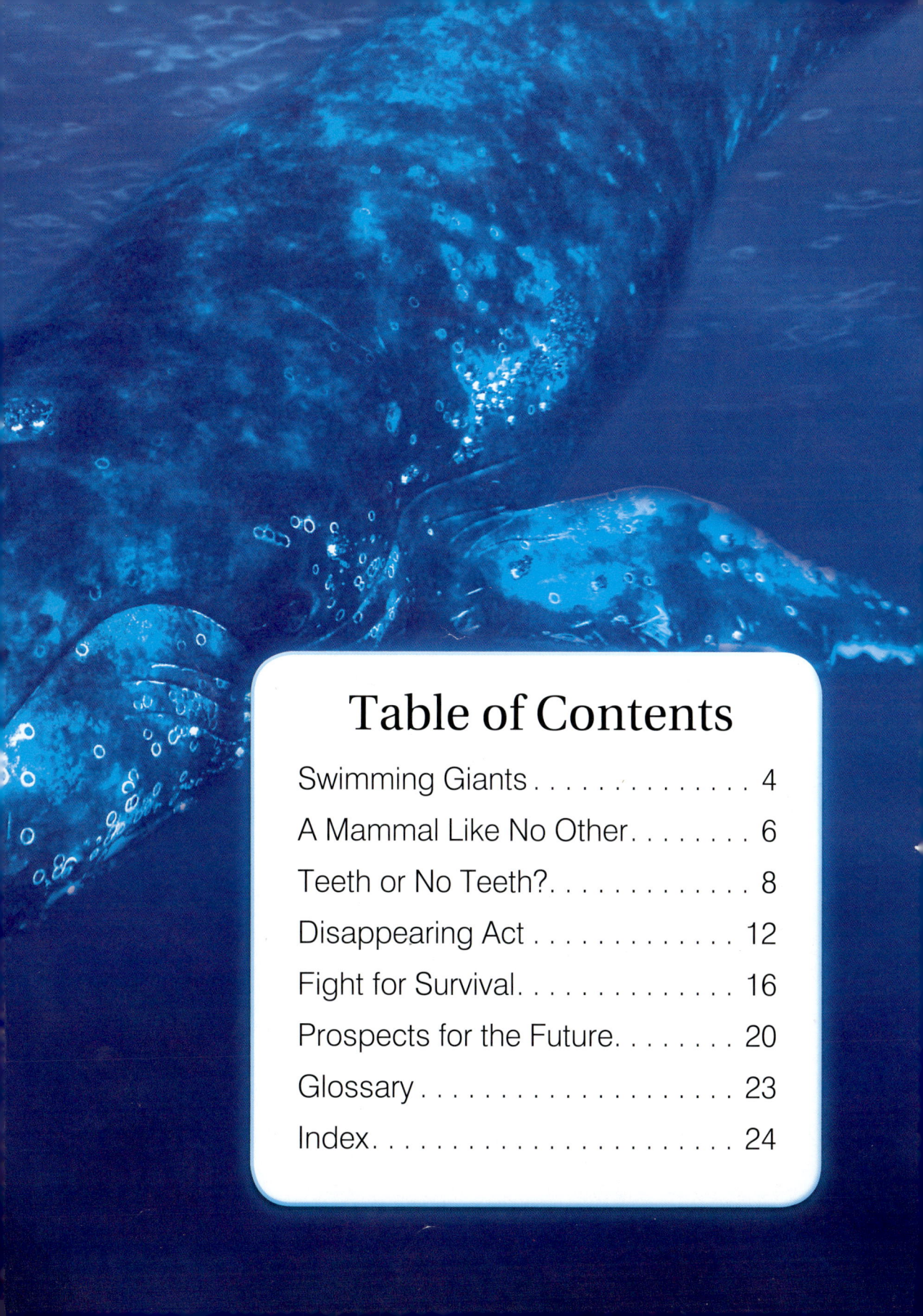

Swimming Giants 4

A Mammal Like No Other 6

Teeth or No Teeth? 8

Disappearing Act 12

Fight for Survival 16

Prospects for the Future 20

Glossary 23

Index 24

Chapter 1
Swimming Giants

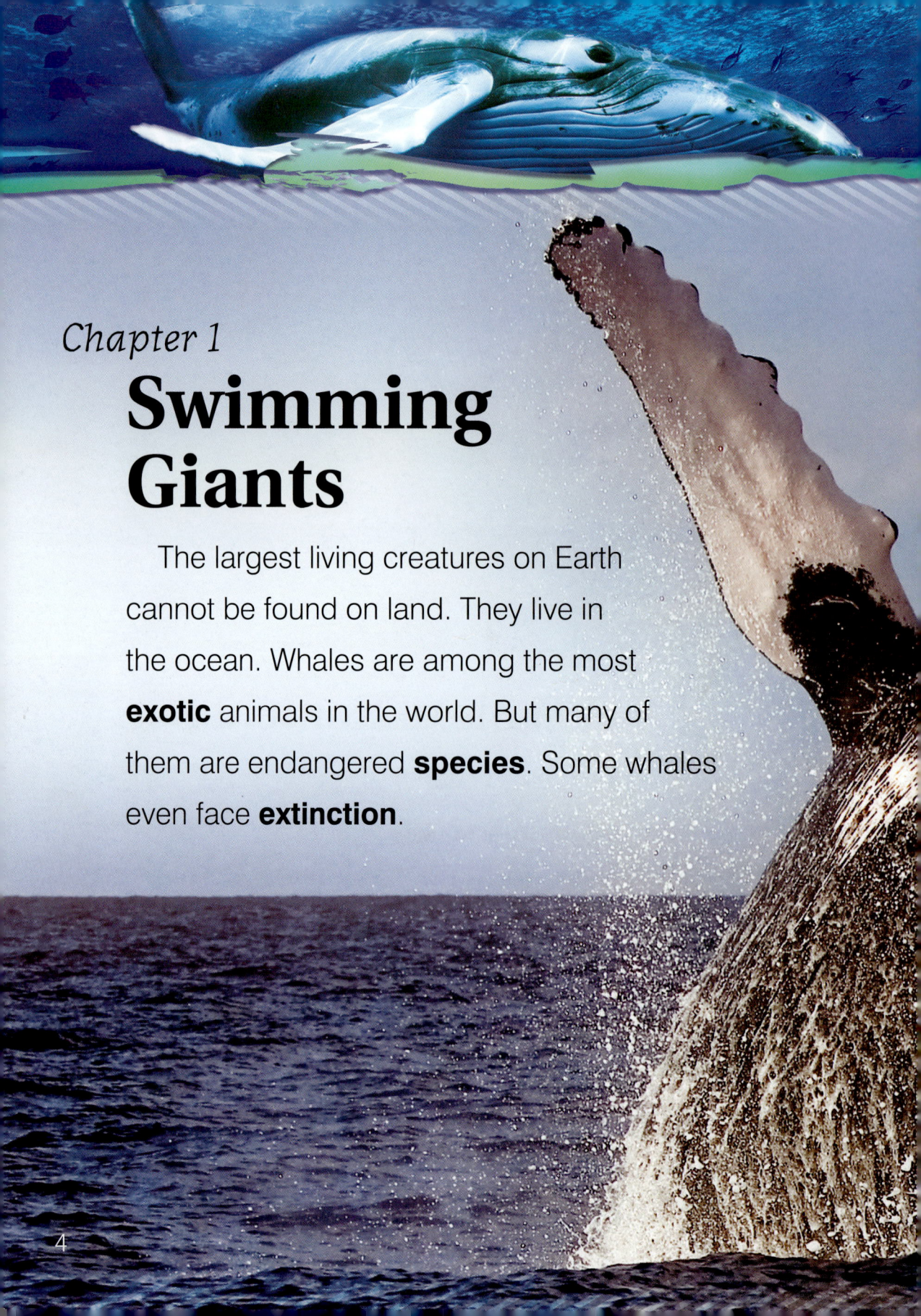

The largest living creatures on Earth cannot be found on land. They live in the ocean. Whales are among the most **exotic** animals in the world. But many of them are endangered **species**. Some whales even face **extinction**.

Whale-watching is a popular tourist activity in some parts of the world.

Chapter 2

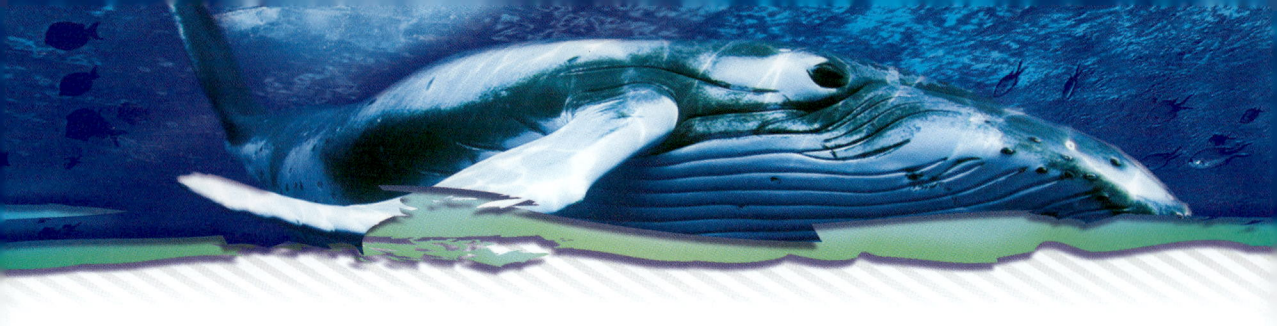

A Mammal Like No Other

Like fish, whales spend their entire lives in the water. Even though they live in the water, whales breathe with lungs, not with **gills**. Whales are mammals. Their baby calves are born live, not hatched from eggs. Whales are warm blooded, but unlike **mammals** living on land, whales rely on **blubber** to stay warm rather than fur.

« *Although much has been learned about whales, scientists continue to study the behavior of these mysterious underwater giants.*

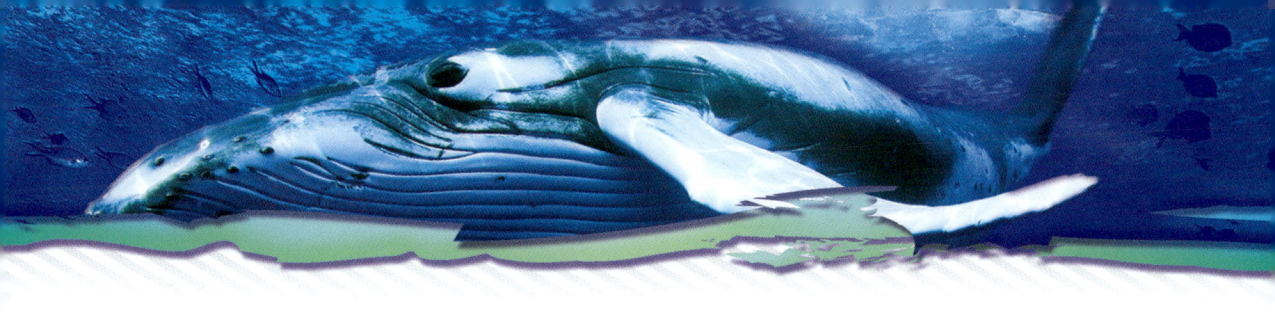

《 Some whales can propel themselves out of the water to splash back down. This is known as breaching.

A whale must swim to the **surface** to breathe through a **blowhole** on top of its head. Air can only get to their lungs through the blowhole. Whales cannot breathe through their mouths.

⌃ When whales exhale, they blow a spout of mist into the air.

Chapter 3

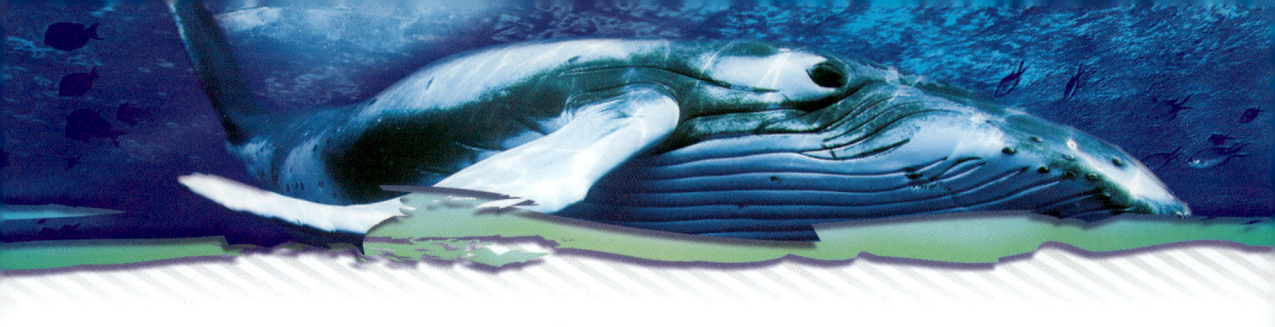

Teeth or No Teeth?

Scientists identify whales in two categories. Whales that have teeth are called toothed whales. Whales that filter their food through flat, flexible plates of bone in their mouths are called **baleen** whales.

The largest toothed whale is the endangered sperm whale. With their huge heads taking up about a third of their length, sperm whales can grow up to 60 feet (18 meters) long.

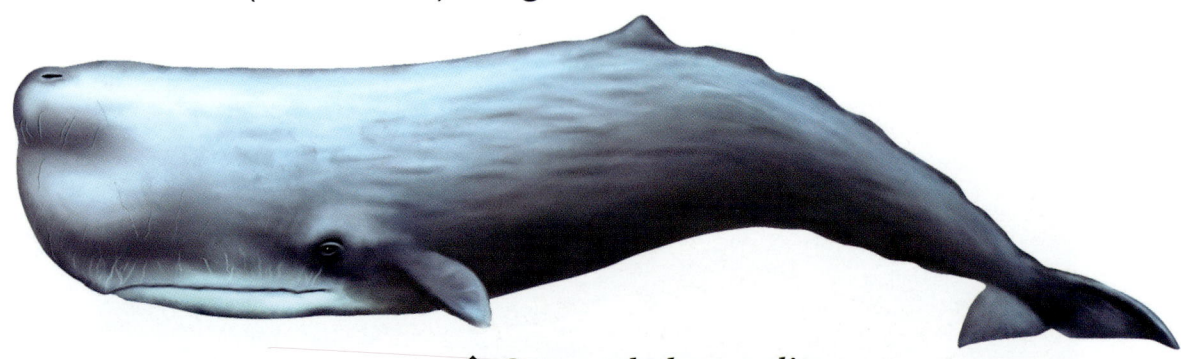

⌃ *Sperm whales can dive more than 3,200 feet (1,000 meters) underwater. No other whale goes that deep.*

⌃ Grey Whale: Baleen whales have two blowholes, located side by side.

⌃ Beluga Whale: Most toothed whales have one blowhole.

One type of endangered baleen whale, the blue whale, is the biggest animal that has ever lived on Earth. It's so big, its heart alone is about the size of a car, and the tongue inside its giant mouth weighs as much as an elephant.

BLUE WHALE

SIZE COMPARISON

A blue whale grows to 100 feet (30 meters) in length. It wouldn't even fit on a full-size basketball court. »

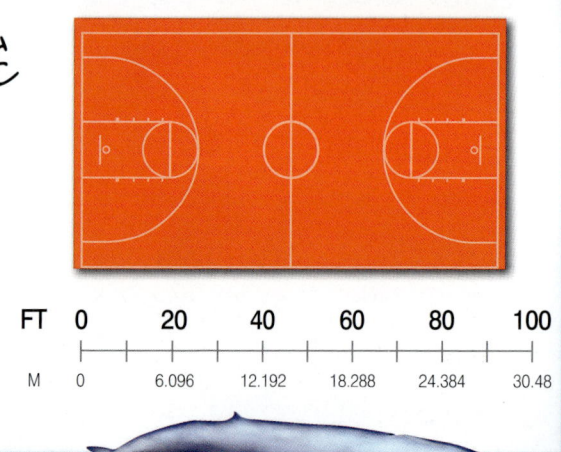

FT	0	20	40	60	80	100
M	0	6.096	12.192	18.288	24.384	30.48

Blue whales are not only the world's biggest animal, they are also the loudest. Their call travels more than 500 miles (800 kilometers) underwater. At 188 **decibels**, its call is far louder than a jet engine.

⌃ *Belugas are known as canaries of the sea. Like canaries, belugas make shrill, high-pitched noises.*

Not all whales are gigantic. The Beluga whale, known by its striking white color, grows to be just 11 to 14 feet (3 to 4.5 meters) long. That's big compared to humans, but not nearly the size of many of its fellow whales. Belugas live in the Arctic Ocean where their skin color often matches their icy **habitat**.

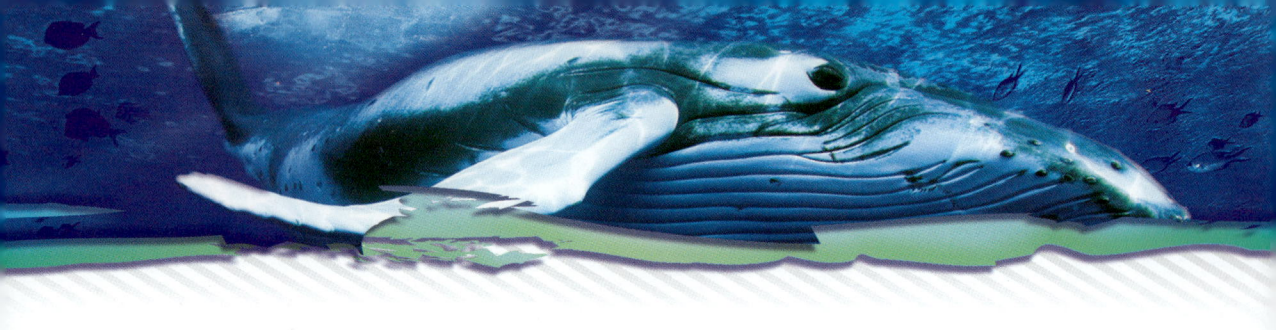

Chapter 4
Disappearing Act

Humans have hunted whales for **centuries** using boats and spears. Later, they used bigger ships and **harpoons**. Then, teams of hunters would watch from shore until a whale would surface, blowing mist from its blowhole.

Commercial Whaling Timeline

1600s | **1700s** | **1800s** | **1900s**

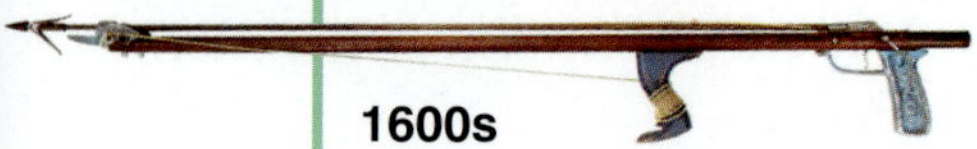

1600s
Whalers use handheld spears called harpoons to kill right, sperm, humpback, and other whales.

1910
Harpoon cannons on larger, faster ships allow whalers to hunt larger whales, including blue whales.

1930s
Right, sperm and humpback whale populations depleted.

1946
International Whaling Commission (IWC) formed.

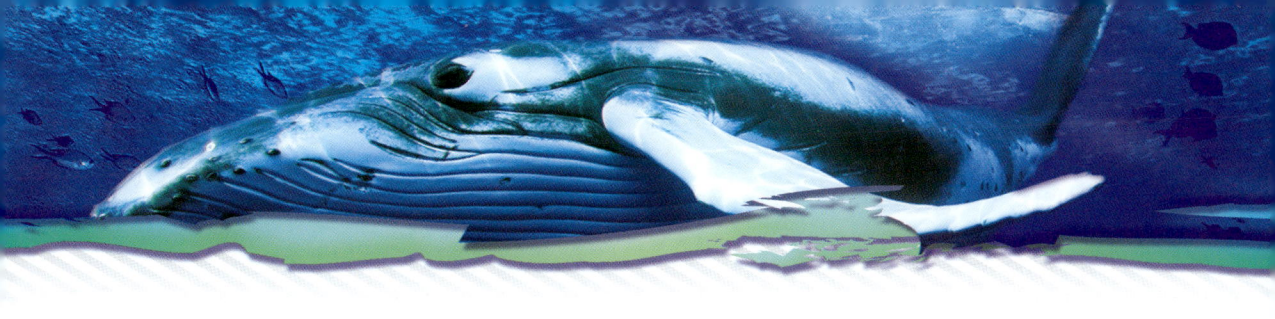

This is the origin of the term "There She Blows." Hunters chased and then killed the whale so they could sell its blubber to make products like soap and cooking oil. Some people even eat whale meat.

《 *Whale hunters are known as whalers.*

1970s to Present
Scientific and **conservation** groups work to halt commercial whaling and protect endangered whales.

1960s
Blue whale population depleted.

PRESENT

1970s
IWC changes focus to protect whales, establishing the first of two massive ocean sanctuaries to protect whales from hunters.

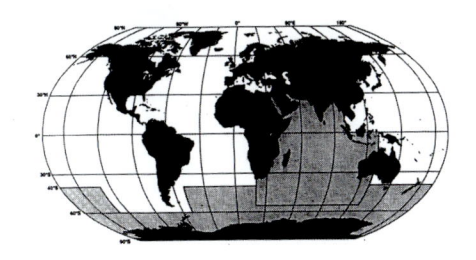

Figure. Boundaries of the Southern Ocean and Indian Ocean Sanctuaries.

13

Professional whalers didn't think the oceans would ever run out of whales, but they were wrong. By the 1930s, some whale **populations** were disappearing.

For centuries, North Atlantic right whales were popular targets for whalers. They were slow swimmers and floated at the surface after being killed. Today, only a few hundred right whales remain.

⌃ The name right whale comes from early whalers. When they were hunting, they called it the "right" whale to catch. If they had said it was the "correct" whale to catch, then the right whale might be named the correct whale!

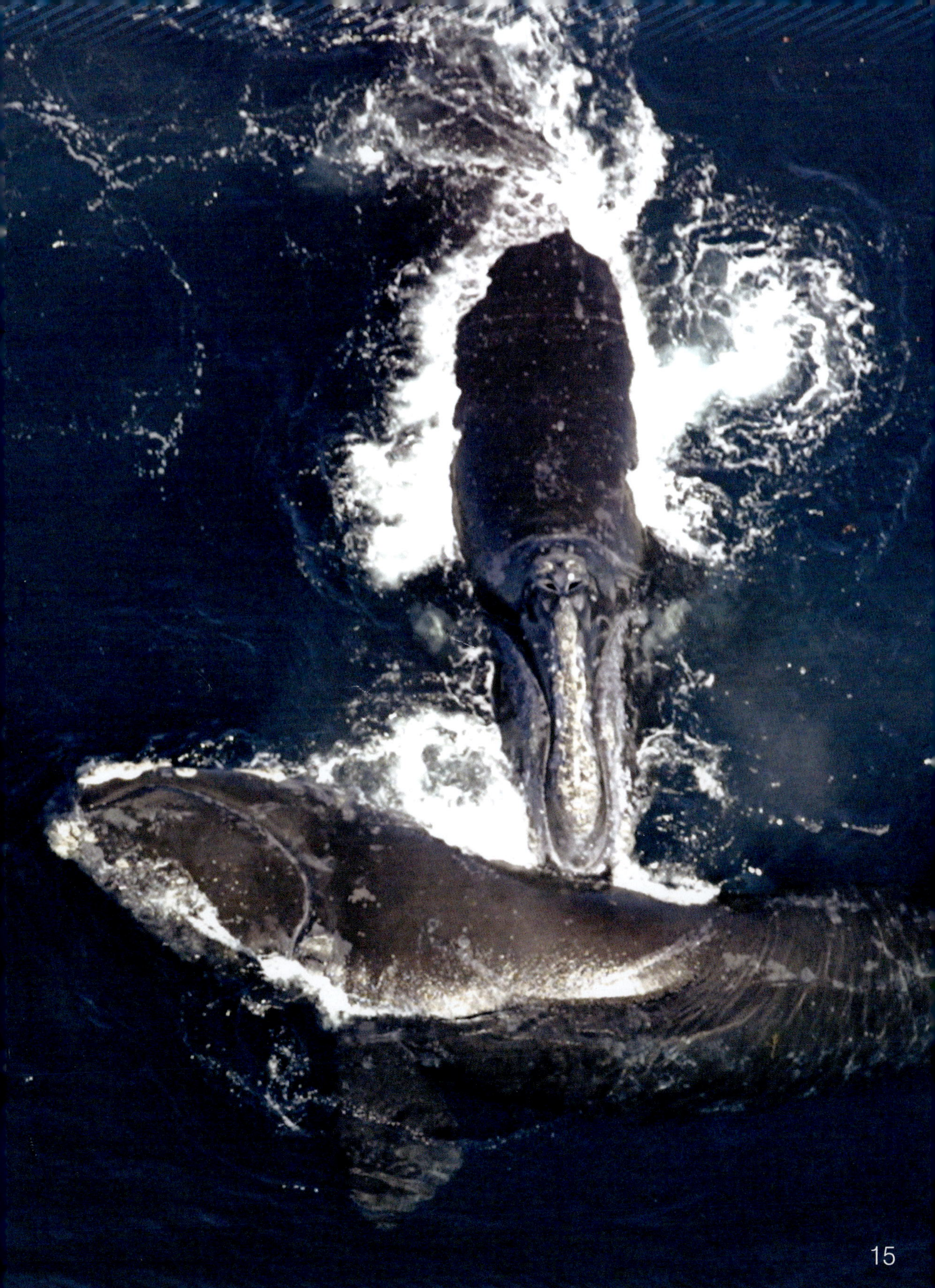

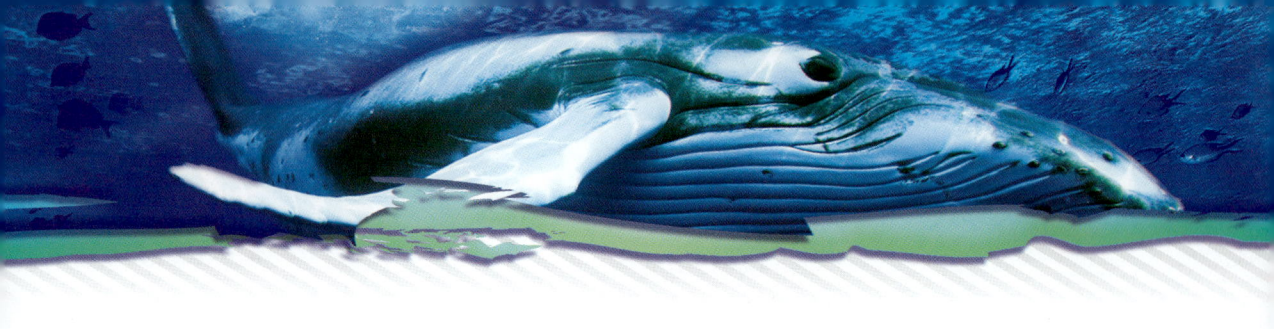

Chapter 6
Fight for Survival

Most countries no longer allow whaling. But endangered whales still face human threats in their ocean habitat. Each year many whales die when they are hit by huge freighters traveling across the ocean.

Large commercial fishing nets kill many whales each year.

Some countries like Japan and Norway, still allow whaling. This practice is controversial and draws criticism from conservation groups.

While whale meat remains a delicacy in Japan, it is illegal to sell it in most countries, including the United States.

17

Two international ocean **sanctuaries** have been established to help whale populations recover. No commercial whaling is allowed inside the Indian Ocean sanctuary or the Southern Ocean sanctuary.

Whale Sanctuaries

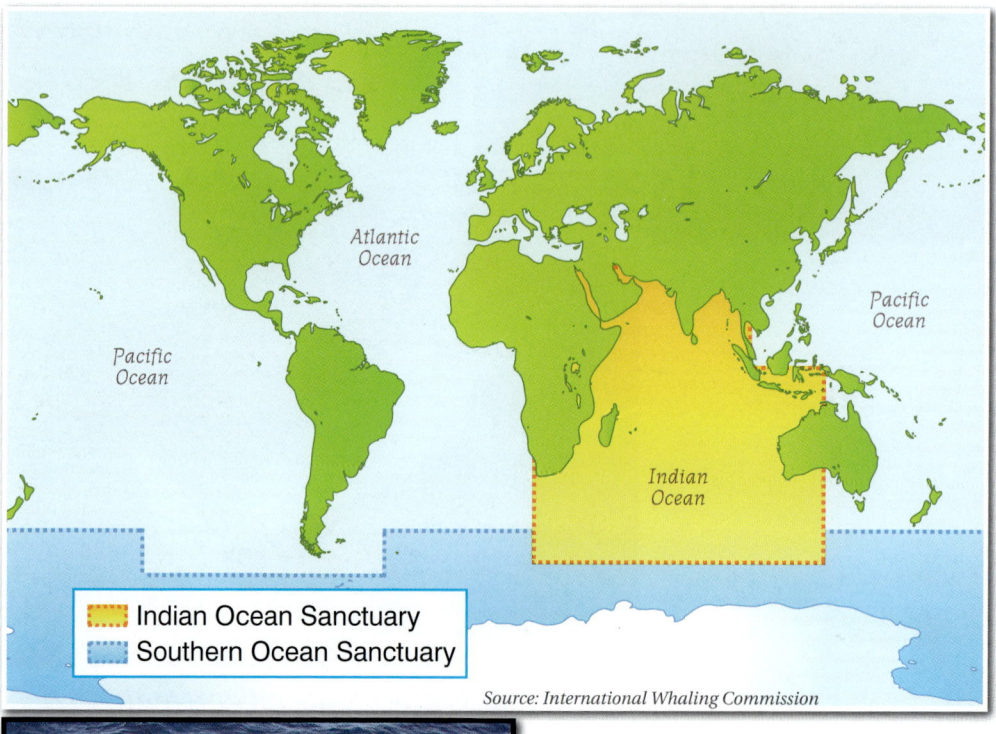

- Indian Ocean Sanctuary
- Southern Ocean Sanctuary

Source: International Whaling Commission

Equipped with unusually long » flippers, humpback whales are among the most active and acrobatic of all whales.

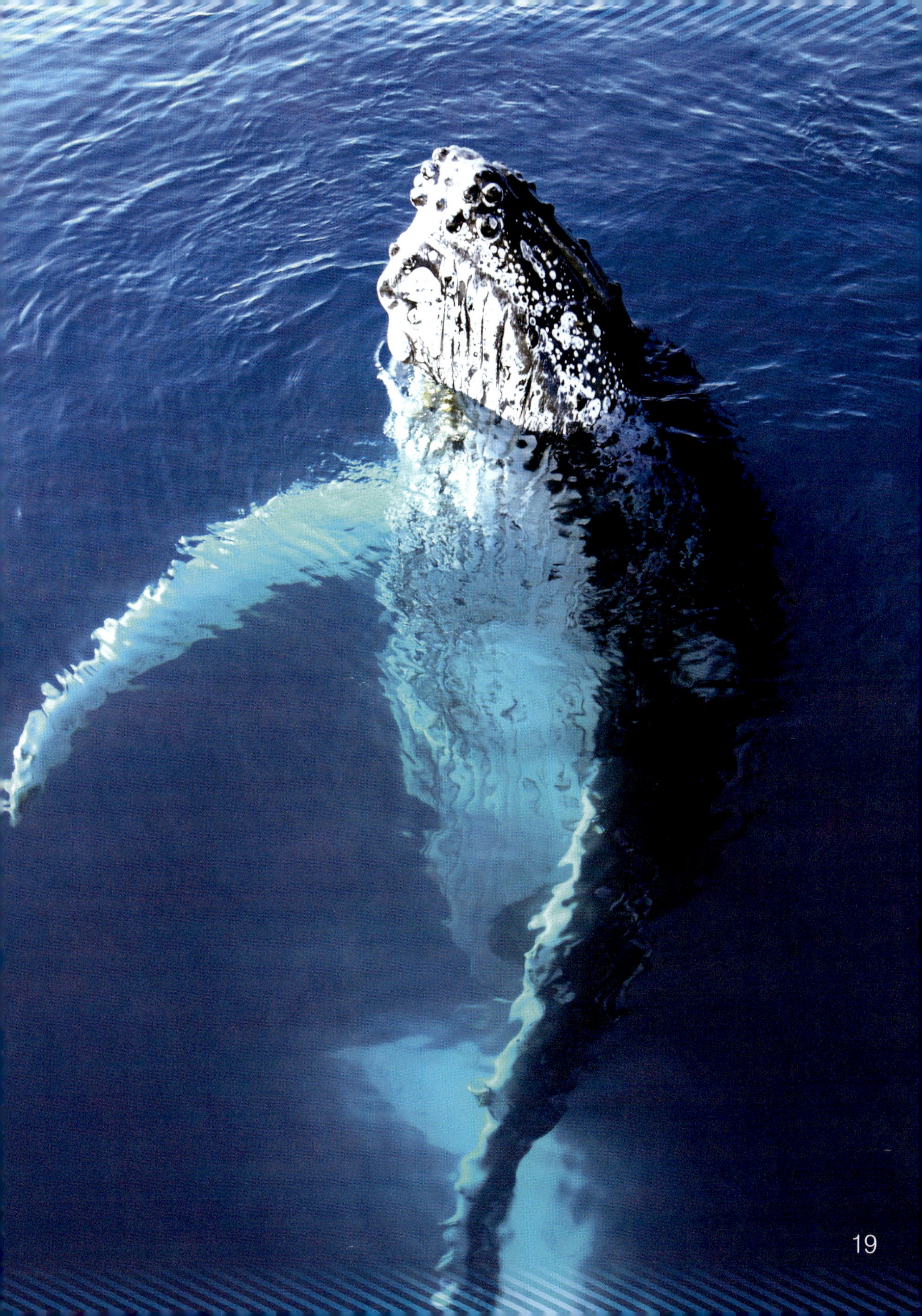

Chapter 7

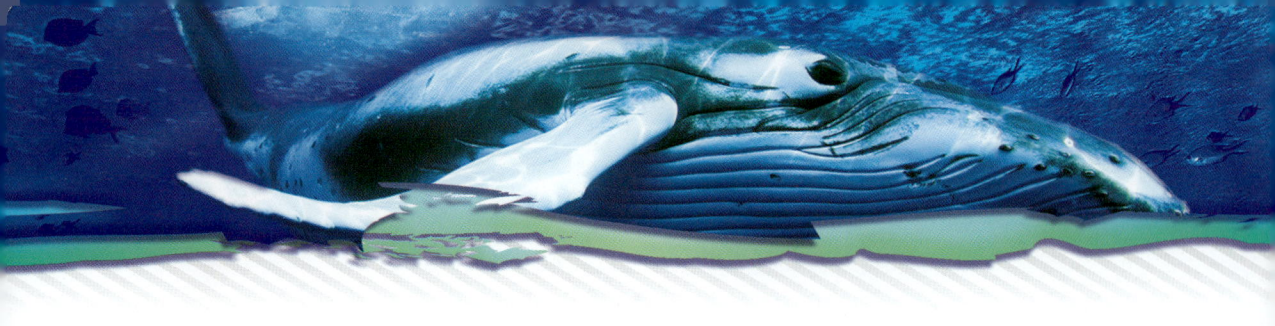

Prospects For the Future

For some endangered whale species, extinction remains a sad possibility. But some whales, once considered endangered, have made a comeback.

Hunted to near extinction by the early 1900s, the California gray whale has rebounded along the North American coast. Hunting them was **banned** worldwide in 1946, and they were removed from the endangered species list in 1994.

⌃ *The flippers at the end of a whales tail are known as its flukes. The flukes of the largest whales can be as big as a small airplane.*

↟ Some gray whales swim all the way from Alaska to Mexico in order to give birth to their calves in warmer waters.

Gray Whale Range

Despite the California gray whale's comeback, Asian gray whales remain endangered, and North Atlantic gray whales are already extinct.

- California Gray Whale
  NO LONGER ENDANGERED
- Asian Gray Whale
  STILL ENDANGERED
- ❌ North Atlantic Gray Whale
  EXTINCT

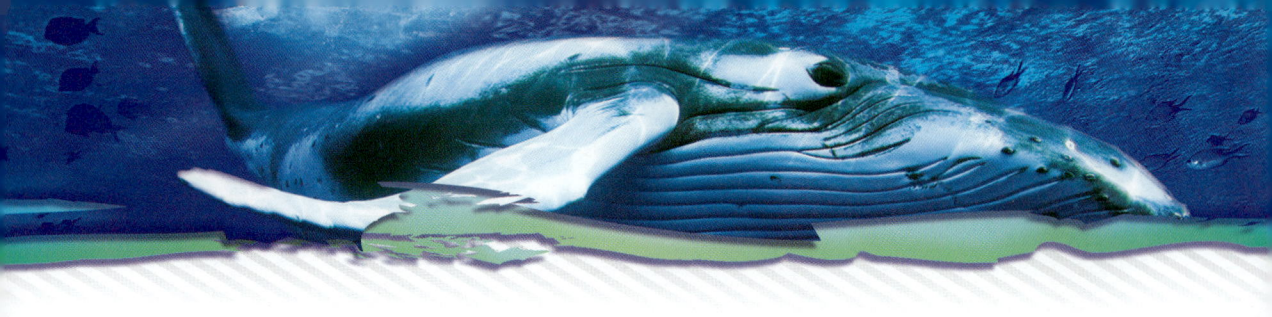

Although no longer widely hunted, whales remain threatened by human factors such as pollution, ship traffic, and fishing nets. People who want to help protect the remaining whales can support or even join whale conservation groups. Scientists and **marine** experts remain **vigilant** to ensure Earth's oceans will be a safe home for whales of all types.

GLOSSARY

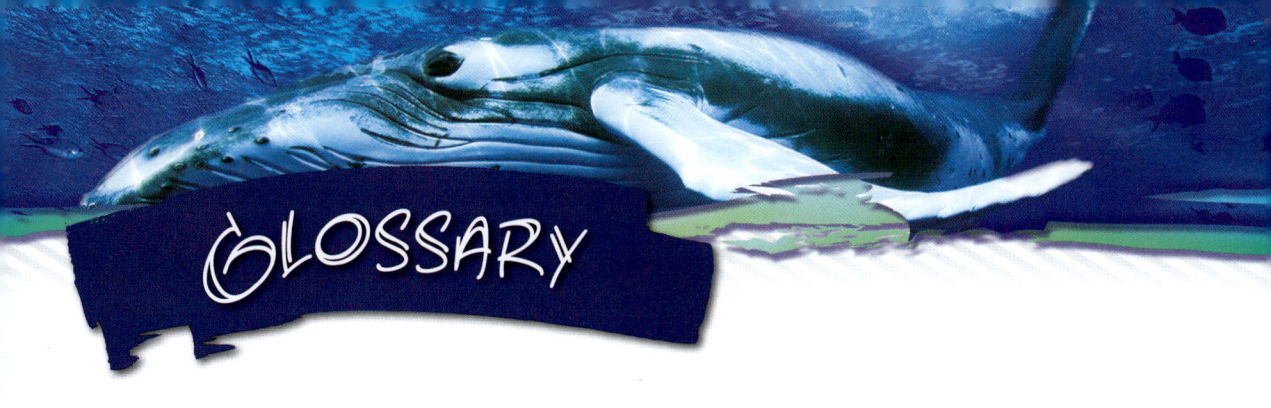

baleen (BAY-leen): special bones inside the mouth of certain whales that filter food from water for the whale to swallow

banned (BAND): something that is not allowed

blowhole (BLOH-hohl): an opening on top of a whale's head that it uses to breathe

blubber (BLUH-bur): thick fat under a whale's skin

centuries (SEN-chuh-reez): a period of 100 years

conservation (kon-sur-VAY-shun): to protect something rare or valuable

decibel (DESS-uh-bel): a unit used to measure the loudness of sounds

exotic (eg-ZOT-ik): strange, interesting

extinction (ek-STINGKT-shun): when an animal dies out and there are no more left living

gills (GILZ): a part of a fish's body that it uses to breathe

habitat (HAB-uh-tat): the place and natural conditions where an animal lives

harpoons (har-POONZ): sharp spears used by whalers to stab whales

mammals (MAM-uhlz): any type of animal that is warm blooded and has a backbone

marine (muh-REEN): living in the ocean

populations (pop-yuh-LAY-shunz): the number of people or animals living in a certain place

sanctuaries (SANGK-choo-er-eez): natural areas where animals are protected from hunters

species (SPEE-seez): a group of related animals

surface (SUR-fiss): the top of a body of water

vigilant (VIJ-uh-luhnt): watchful and alert

Index

baleen   8, 9, 10
blue whale(s)   10, 11, 12, 13
breathe   6, 7
conservation   13, 17, 22
fishing   22
gray whale(s)   20, 21
hunting   14, 20
population(s)   12, 13, 14
right whale(s)   14
size   10, 11
sperm whale(s)   8
toothed   8, 9
tourist   5

Websites to Visit

animals.nationalgeographic.com/animals/mammals/blue-whale.html

www.worldwildlife.org/species/finder/cetaceans/whalesanddolphins.html

www.neaq.org/conservation_and_research/projects/endangered_species_habitats/right_whale_research/index.php

www.savethewhales.org

About the Author

Tom Greve lives in Chicago with his wife Meg and their children Madison and William. He loves the outdoors, and finds the Earth's oceans fascinating.